GREENB

* Numerical *
Pocket Price Guide and Inventory Checklist to

AMERICAN FLYER®
S GAUGE

Edited by Marcy Damon

Manufactured in the United States of America

Greenberg Publishing Company, Inc. publishes the world's largest selection of Lionel, American Flyer, LGB, Marx, Ives, and other toy train publications as well as a selection of books on model and prototype railroading, dollhouse building, and collectible toys. For a complete listing of current Greenberg publications, please call 1-800-533-6644 (Fax orders: 414-796-0126) or write to Kalmbach Publishing, 21027 Crossroads Circle, Waukesha, WI 53187.

Greenberg Shows, Inc. sponsors *Greenberg's Great Train, Dollhouse and Toy Shows*, the world's largest of its kind. The shows feature extravagant operating train layouts, and a display of magnificent dollhouses. The shows also present a huge marketplace of model and toy trains, for HO, N, and Z Scales; Lionel O and Standard Gauges; and S and 1 Gauges; plus layout accessories and railroadiana. It also offers a large selection of dollhouse miniatures and building materials, and collectible toys. Shows are scheduled along the East Coast each year from Massachusetts to Florida. For a list of our current shows please call (301) 795-7447 or write to the Maryland address below and request a show brochure.

Greenberg Auctions, a division of Greenberg Shows, Inc., offers nationally advertised auctions of toy trains and toys. Please contact our auction manager at (301) 795-7447 for further information.

Eighth Edition

Greenberg Publishing Company, Inc.
7566 Main Street
Sykesville, Maryland 21784

TABLE OF CONTENTS

INTRODUCTION

This revised **Pocket Price Guide** has been completely reset in larger type for easier reading. It lists all major AMERICAN FLYER S GAUGE items built by the A. C. Gilbert Company or by Lionel Trains, Inc. The price quoted is for the most common variety of each item. Some varieties are worth considerably more. There are some rare varieties cited. Some newly manufactured items made by Lionel may not have well established prices; they are marked "CP" for current production. For additional information on all S Gauge items, please consult the comprehensive *Greenberg's Guide to American Flyer S Gauge, Volumes I* and *II* (described on the rear cover).

Dates cited are catalogued dates. If there is no catalogue date, production dates are listed if known. American Flyer often listed "Built Dates" on its equipment. These may or may not coincide with the actual catalogue or production dates.

Train values in this **Pocket Price Guide** are based on prices obtained at large train meets from 1991. The prices reported here represent a "ready sale," or a price perceived as a good value by the buyer. These prices sometimes appear lower than those seen on trains for sale at meets for two reasons. First, items that do sell often sell quickly in the first hour of a train meet and, therefore, are no longer visible. (We have observed that a considerable amount of action usually occurs in the first hour.) The items that do not sell in the first hour have a higher price tag and this price, although not representing the sales price, is the price observed at the meet. A related source of discrepancy is the willingness of some sellers to bargain over price.

From our studies of train prices, it appears that mail order prices for used trains are generally higher than those obtained at train meets. This is quite appropriate considering the cost and effort of producing and distributing a price list and packing and shipping items. Mail order items do sell at prices above those listed in this book.

As we indicated, prices in this book were derived from large train meets or shows. If you sell your trains to a person planning to resell them at another train meet, you will not obtain the prices reported in this book. Rather, you will probably receive about fifty percent of these prices. Basically, for your trains to be of interest to a buyer who plans to resell them, he must purchase them for considerably less than the prices listed here. We receive inquiries as to whether or not a particular piece is a "good value." This book will help you answer that question; but there is NO substitute for experience in the marketplace. WE STRONGLY RECOMMEND THAT NOVICES DO NOT MAKE MAJOR PURCHASES WITHOUT THE ASSISTANCE OF FRIENDS WHO HAVE EXPERIENCE IN BUYING AND SELLING TRAINS.

DEFINITIONS

This **Pocket Price Guide** defines prices for GOOD and EXCELLENT (or MINT). Prices for restored pieces fall between Good and Excellent depending on the item. Mint pieces bring a substantial premium over Excellent pieces. Fair pieces bring substantially less than Good pieces.

Trains and related items are usually classified by condition. The categories are defined as:

FAIR — Well-scratched, chipped, dented, rusted, or warped.

GOOD — Scratches, small dents, dirty.

VERY GOOD — Few scratches, exceptionally clean, no dents or rust.

EXCELLENT — Minute scratches or nicks, no dents or rust, all original with less than average wear.

LIKE NEW — Only the faintest signs of handling and wheel wear with crisp, vibrant colors that show no evidence of polishing.

MINT — Brand new, absolutely unmarred, all original and unused, with no evidence of being handled.

RESTORED — Professionally refinished to a color that very closely approximates the original finish, all trim and ornamental features are present, and the item has a like-new appearance.

NRS — **N**o **R**eported **S**ales — Means the editors did not have sufficient information to establish a price. This usually indicates that the item is scarce. Therefore sales have not been reported. We appreciate all reports from readers on those items labeled NRS. **Note:** An item labeled NRS does not **always** secure a high price. Extreme caution is advised when purchasing any item marked NRS for a substantial sum.

CP — **C**urrent **P**roduction means that the item is either now being manufactured or is currently available from retail stores.

In the toy train field there is a great deal of concern with exterior appearance and less concern with operation. If operation is important to you, you should ask the seller if the train runs. If the seller indicates that he does not know whether the equipment operates, you should test it. Most train meets provide test tracks for this purpose.

Item numbers listed in parentheses do not appear on the cars.

No number means the item may have lettering but lacks an item number.

No lettering means the item has no lettering or number on the car.

Reproductions
By Jim Patterson

The following items have been reproduced or created by repainting other items; some reproductions are marked and some are not. A scratch in the black lettering will show the original color underneath.

Diesels:
Boston and Maine
467 Comet, B unit
476 Rocket, B unit
490/491/493 NP
21920, 21920-1 MP
21925, 21925-1 UP

Passenger Sets:
900, 901, 902, 903 NP
24837, 24838, 24839, 24840 UP
24856, 24859, 24863, 24866 MP

Boxcars:
G. Fox & Co.
C1001 WSX
(24067) Keystone
24068 Planters Peanut
(24420) Simmons

Chemically Altered Boxcars:
622 GAEX
623 Illinois Central
637 MKT
802 Illinois Central
922 GAEX
923 Illinois Central
937 MKT
24403 Illinois Central

Accessories:
594 Track Gang

Covered Hopper:
24222 Domino Sugar

Flatcars:
The loads on flatcars have been reproduced.
643 AF Circus, loads reproduced
(245)65 FY & PRR, cannons reproduced

Tank Cars:
910 Gilbert Chemical – production item was Gilbert
24319 Pennsylvania Salt

NUMERICAL LISTINGS
Gilbert Production

	Good	Exc	Cond / $
American Flyer Circus See (649)			
"Borden's" Pike Master couplers. See (24575)			
Boston and Maine PA*	NRS	NRS	_____
Buffalo Hunt Gondola, 1963	3	10	_____
C & NWRY 42597 With link couplers. See (628)			
C & NWRY 42597 With knuckle couplers. See (928) or 934			
Freight Ahead Caboose, 1963	2	7	_____
G. Fox & Co. See (633F)			
Keystone See (24067)			
New Haven With pipes, Pike Master couplers. See (24564)			
Pennsylvania See (24130)			
Rocket Launcher and USM See (25056)			
Simmons See (24420)			
Undecorated body Flatcar	1	3	_____
Virginian See (632)			
Washington See (21089)			
1 25-watt transformer, 1950-52	.50	2	_____
1 35-watt transformer, 1956	1	4	_____
1A 40-watt transformer, 1957 (U)	1	4	_____
1½ 45-watt transformer, 1953	1	3	_____
1½ 50-watt transformer, 1954-55	1	3	_____
1½B 50-watt transformer, 1956	1	3	_____
2 75-watt transformer, 1947-52	1	3	_____
2B 75-watt transformer, 1948	2	6	_____
3 50-watt transformer, 1946 (U)	1	3	_____
4B 100-watt transformer, 1949-56	2	9	_____
5 50-watt transformer, 1946	1	4	_____
5A 50-watt transformer, 1946	1	4	_____
5B 50-watt transformer, 1946	2	6	_____
6 75-watt transformer, 1946	1	4	_____
6A 75-watt transformer, 1946	.50	2	_____
7B 75-watt transformer, 1946	2	6	_____
8B 100-watt transformer, 1946-52	6	15	_____
9B 150-watt transformer, 1946	10	20	_____
10 DC invertor, 1946	3	10	_____
11 Circuit breaker, 1946	3	10	_____
12B 250-watt transformer, 1946-52	15	45	_____
13 Circuit breaker, 1952-55	3	7	_____
14 Rectiformer, 1947, 1949	8	25	_____
15 Rectifier, 1948-52	5	15	_____
15B 110-watt transformer, 1953	10	20	_____

	Good	Exc	Cond / $
16 Rectiformer, 1950	5	30	_____
16B 190-watt transformer, 1953	15	45	_____
16C 35-watt transformer, 1958	6	15	_____
17B 190-watt transformer, 1952	20	50	_____
18 Filter, 1950 (U)	NRS	NRS	_____
18B 175-watt transformer, 1953	20	50	_____
18B 190-watt transformer, 1953	20	50	_____
19B 300-watt transformer, 1952-55	30	80	_____
20 See (247)20			
21 Imitation grass, 1949-50	3	8	_____
21A Imitation grass, 1951-56	3	8	_____
22 Scenery gravel, 1949-56	3	8	_____
23 Artificial coal, 1949-56	3	8	_____
24 Rainbow wire, 1949-56	2	6	_____
25 Smoke cartridge, 1947-56	2	6	_____
26 Service kit, 1952-56	4	15	_____
27 Track cleaning fluid, 1952-56	2	4	_____
28 Track ballast, 1950	4	10	_____
28A Track ballast, 1951-53	4	10	_____
29 Imitation snow, 1950	10	45	_____
29A Imitation snow, 1951-53	10	45	_____
30 Highway signs, 1949-52	20	90	_____
30 See (247)30			
30B 300-watt transformer, 1953-56	35	80	_____
31 Railroad signs, 1949-50	30	100	_____
31A Railroad signs, 1951-52	30	100	_____
32 City street equipment, 1949-50	25	90	_____
32A Park set, 1951	25	110	_____
33 Pass. and train figure set, 1951-52	30	100	_____
34 Railway figure set, 1953	25	425	_____
35 Brakeman with lantern, 1950-52	25	75	_____
40 See (247)40			
40 Smoke set, 1953-55	2	4	_____
50 District school, 1953-54	25	105	_____
50 See (247)50			
55 See (240)55			
65 See (245)65			
88 See (210)88			
100 Step display, 1948	NRS	NRS	_____
100 Universal lock-on	NRS	NRS	_____
160 Station platform, 1953	30	100	_____
161 Bungalow, 1953	25	100	_____
162 Factory, 1953	30	130	_____
163 Flyerville station, 1953	30	130	_____
164 Red barn, 1953	35	150	_____
165 Grain elevator, 1953	40	150	_____
166 Church, 1953	40	140	_____

		Good	Exc	Cond / $
167	Town hall, 1953	35	140	_____
168	Hotel, 1953	35	140	_____
234	See (21)234			
247	Tunnel, 1946-48	15	30	_____
248	Tunnel, 1946-48	15	30	_____
249	Tunnel, 1947-56	3	30	_____
263	PRR, 0-6-0, switcher, 1957		Not produced	
270	News and frank stand, 1952-53	20	70	_____
271	Three-piece "Whistle Stop" set, 1952-53	NRS	75	_____
	1) Waiting station	12	25	_____
	2) Refreshment booth	12	25	_____
	3) Newsstand	12	25	_____
272	Glendale station and newsstand, 1952-53	30	85	_____
273	Suburban railroad station, 1952-53	30	70	_____
274	Harbor Jct. freight station, 1952-53	30	75	_____
275	Eureka diner, 1952-53	30	75	_____
282	CNW, 4-6-2, Pacific, 1952-53			
	(A) 1952, "American Flyer"	20	55	_____
	(B) 1953, with coal pusher	25	70	_____
283	CNW, 4-6-2, Pacific, 1954-57	15	60	_____
285	CNW, 4-6-2, Pacific, 1952	35	140	_____
287	CNW, 4-6-2, Pacific, 1954	20	80	_____
289	CNW, 4-6-2, Pacific, 1956 (U)	60	225	_____
290	AF, 4-6-2, Pacific, 1949-51	20	60	_____
292	CNW, 4-6-2, Pacific, 1952 (U)	NRS	NRS	_____
293	NYNH & H, 4-6-2, Pacific, 1953-58			
	(A) 1953-57, reverse in tender	20	85	_____
	(B) 1957 (U), reverse in cab	NRS	NRS	_____
295	AF, 4-6-2, Pacific, 1951	50	200	_____
296	NYNH & H, 4-6-2, Pacific, 1955 (U)	60	250	_____
299	RL, 4-4-2, Atlantic, 1954	40	150	_____
300	Reading, 4-4-2, Atlantic, 1946-47, 1952			
	(A) 1946-47, "Reading"	15	60	_____
	(B) 1947, 1952, other variations	10	40	_____
300 AC	RL, 4-4-2, Atlantic, 1949-50	10	35	_____
301	RL, 4-4-2, Atlantic, 1953	10	35	_____
302	Reading Lines, 4-4-2, Atlantic, mv, 1948, 1951-53	10	40	_____
302 AC	Reading Lines, 4-4-2, Atlantic, mv, 1948, 1951-52	10	40	_____
303	RL, 4-4-2, Atlantic, 1954-56	10	40	_____
307	RL, 4-4-2, Atlantic, 1954-57	10	25	_____
308	RL, 4-4-2, Atlantic, 1956	15	75	_____
310	PRR, 4-6-2, Pacific, 1946-48	20	80	_____

	Good	Exc	Cond / $
312 PRR, 4-6-2, Pacific, mv, 1946, 1948, 1951-52			
(A) 1946, sit., "Pennsylvania"	30	110	_____
(B) Other variations	25	100	_____
312 AC PRR, 4-6-2, Pacific, 1949-51	30	110	_____
313 PRR, 4-6-2, Pacific, 1955-56	40	150	_____
314AW PRR, 4-6-2, Pacific, 1949-50	60	245	_____
315 PRR, 4-6-2, Pacific, 1952	40	155	_____
316 PRR, 4-6-2, Pacific, 1953-54	40	175	_____
320 NYC, 4-6-4, Hudson, 1946-47	35	120	_____
321 NYC, 4-6-4, Hudson, 1946-47	45	180	_____
322 NYC, 4-6-4, Hudson, 1946-50			
(A) 1946, "New York Central"	35	125	_____
(B) 1947-4, "American Flyer Lines"	30	110	_____
322AC NYC, 4-6-4, Hudson, 1949-50	35	125	_____
324AC NYC, 4-6-4, Hudson, 1950	40	160	_____
325AC NYC, 4-6-4, Hudson, 1951	35	140	_____
K325 NYC, 4-6-4, Hudson, 1952			
(A) Early coupler riveted to truck	40	160	_____
(B) Other variations	35	135	_____
326 NYC, 4-6-4, Hudson, 1953-57	40	155	_____
332 UP, 4-8-4, Northern, 1946-49			
(A) 1946, AC, sit., "Union Pacific"	NRS	NRS	_____
(B) 1948, AC, "American Flyer Lines"	75	275	_____
(C) 1948-49, DC, "American Flyer Lines"	75	280	_____
(D) 1947, DC, silver lettering	NRS	1500	
332AC UP, 4-8-4, Northern, 1950-51	80	300	_____
332DC UP, 4-8-4, Northern, 1950 (U)	80	375	_____
334DC UP, 4-8-4, Northern, 1950	100	400	_____
K335 UP, 4-8-4, Northern, 1952	75	300	_____
336 UP, 4-8-4, Northern, 1953-56	100	400	_____
342 Nickel Plate Road, 0-8-0, switcher, 1946-48, 1952			
(A) 1946, sit., "Nickel Plate Road"	NRS	NRS	_____
(B) 1947, sit., "American Flyer Lines"	100	400	_____
(C) Same as (B), but DC	110	475	_____
(D) 1948, sib., "American Flyer Lines"	75	300	_____
342AC NKP, 0-8-0, switcher, 1949-51	70	275	_____
342DC NKP, 0-8-0, switcher, 1948-50	65	250	_____
343 Nickel Plate Road, 0-8-0, switcher, 1953-58			
(A) 1953-54, reverse in tender	75	300	_____
(B) 1954, 1956, reverse on motor	90	350	_____
346 NKP, 0-8-0, switcher, 1955	125	500	_____
350 Royal Blue, 4-6-2, Pacific, mv, 1948, 1950			
(A) 1948, wire handrails	25	95	_____
(B) 1950, cast handrails	25	95	_____
353 AF Circus, 4-6-2, Pacific, 1950-51	90	375	_____
354 Silver Bullet, 4-6-2, Pacific, 1954	30	115	_____

	Good	Exc	Cond / $
355 CNW, Baldwin, 1956-57			
(A) Unpainted green plastic	40	100	____
(B) Green-painted plastic	NRS	NRS	____
356 Silver Bullet, 4-6-2, Pacific, 1953	35	150	____
360/361 SF, PA/PB, 1950-51			
(A) 1950, chromed	50	200	____
(B) 1950, chromed with handrails	100	450	____
(C) 1951, silver-painted	35	150	____
360/364 SF, PA/PB, 1950-51			
(A) 1951, silver-painted, "Santa Fe"	40	150	____
(B) Other variations	NRS	NRS	____
370 GM AF, GP-7, 1950-53			
(A) With link coupler bars	35	110	____
(B) With knuckle couplers	35	110	____
371 GM AF, GP-7, 1954	60	135	____
372 UP, GP-7, 1955-57			
(A) "Built by Gilbert"	100	200	____
(B) "Made by American Flyer"	100	250	____
374/375 T & P, GP-7, 1955			
(A) Sheet metal frame	175	400	____
(B) Die-cast frame	160	375	____
375 GM AF, GP-7, 1953	400	1200	____
377/378 T & P, GP-7, 1956-57	150	425	____
(405) Silver Streak, PA, 1952	60	175	____
440 Lamp	1	3	____
441 Lamp	1	3	____
442 Lamp	1	3	____
443 Lamp	1	3	____
444 Lamp	1	3	____
450 Track terminal, 1946-48	1	3	____
451 Lamp	1	3	____
452 Lamp	1	3	____
453 Lamp, 1946-48	1	3	____
460 Bulbs, 1951, 1953-54	10	55	____
461 Lamp	2	8	____
466 Comet, PA, 1953-55			
(A) 1953, chromed	90	250	____
(B) 1954-55, silver-painted, decal	90	200	____
(C) Same as (B) w/heat-stamped lett.	90	275	____
467 Comet, PB, 1955*	NRS	7000	____
470/471/473 SF, PA/PB/PA, 1953-57			
(A) 1953, chromed	120	375	____
(B) 1954-57, silver-painted	100	325	____
(C) Silver-painted, integral steps	200	500	____
472 Santa Fe, PA, 1956	80	200	____

	Good	Exc	Cond / $
474/475 Rocket, PA/PA, 1953-55			
(A) 1953, chromed	100	300	____
(B) 1954-55, silver-painted	90	270	____
476 Rocket, PB, 1955*	NRS	NRS	____
477/478 Silver Flash, PA/PB, 1953-54			
(A) 1953, chromed	150	450	____
(B) 1954, silver-painted	150	450	____
479 Silver Flash, PA, 1955	60	225	____
480 Silver Flash, PB, 1955*	NRS	1000	____
481 Silver Flash, PA, 1956	90	275	____
484/485/486 SF, PA/PB/PA, 1956-57	175	550	____
490/491/493 NP, PA/PB/PA, 1956*	350	1500	____
490/492 NP, PA/PA, 1957	200	750	____
494/495 NH, PA/PA, 1956	200	850	____
497 New Haven, PA, 1957	100	300	____
499 NH, GE electric, 1956-57	125	475	____
500 AF Lines, combination, 1952 (U)			
(A) Silver finish	100	425	____
(B) Chrome finish	75	300	____
501 AF Lines, coach, 1952 (U)			
(A) Silver finish	125	425	____
(B) Chrome finish	QE	QE	____
502 AFL passenger car, vista dome, 1952 (U)			
(A) Silver finish	100	425	____
(B) Chrome finish	75	300	____
503 AF Lines, observation, 1952 (U)			
(A) Silver finish	100	425	____
(B) Chrome finish	QE	QE	____
520 Knuckle coupler kit, 1954-56	2	5	____
521 Knuckle coupler kit	NRS	NRS	____
525 Knuckle coupler trucks	NRS	NRS	____
526 Knuckle coupler trucks	NRS	NRS	____
529 Knuckle coupler trucks	NRS	NRS	____
530 Knuckle coupler trucks	NRS	NRS	____
532 Knuckle coupler trucks	NRS	NRS	____
541 Fuses, 1946	NRS	NRS	____
561 Billboard horn, 1955-56	12	30	____
566 Whistling billboard, 1951-55	10	25	____
568 Whistling billboard, 1956	10	25	____
571 Truss bridge, 1955-56	3	12	____
573 AF talking station record	NRS	NRS	____
577 Whistling billboard, 1946-50			
(A) 1946-47, circus	8	25	____
(B) 1946, typewriter	8	25	____
(C) 1947, Fox Mart	NRS	NRS	____
578 Station figure set, 1946-52	30	75	____
579 Single street lamp, 1946-49	4	10	____

	Good	Exc	Cond / $
580 Double street lamp, 1946-49	5	12	_____
581 Girder bridge, 1946-56	2	15	_____
582 Blinker signal, 1946-48	15	40	_____
583 Electromatic crane, 1946-49	20	75	_____
583A Electromatic crane, 1950-53	20	90	_____
584 Bell danger signal, 1946-47	40	150	_____
585 Tool shed, 1946-52	10	30	_____
586F Wayside station, 1946-56	15	40	_____
587 Block signal, 1946-47	20	75	_____
588 Semaphore block signal, 1946-48	NRS	NRS	_____
589 Passenger and freight station, 1946-56			
(A) Green-painted roof	10	40	_____
(B) Black-painted roof	15	45	_____
590 Control tower, 1955-56	15	50	_____
591 Crossing gate, 1946-48	20	50	_____
592 Crossing gate, 1949-50	10	35	_____
592A Crossing gate, 1951-53	10	35	_____
593 Signal tower, 1946-54	18	60	_____
594 Animated track gang, 1946-47*	500	2000	_____
596 Water tank, 1946-56	15	55	_____
598 Talking station record, 1946-56	8	15	_____
599 Talking station record, 1956	6	30	_____
600 Crossing gate with bell, 1954-56	10	35	_____
605 AF Lines, flatcar, 1953	5	25	_____
606 AF Lines, crane, 1953	10	30	_____
607 AF Lines, work and boom car, 1953	5	22	_____
609 AF Lines, flatcar, 1953	5	25	_____
612 Freight passenger station crane, 1946-51, 1953-54	25	60	_____
613 Great Northern, boxcar, 1953	7	20	_____
620 Southern, gondola, 1953	7	30	_____
621 ½ straight track, 1946-48	.20	.50	_____
622 ½ curve track, 1946-48	.20	.50	_____
622 GAEX, boxcar, 1953*	8	35	_____
623 Illinois Central, reefer, 1953*	6	14	_____
625 Shell, tank car, 1946-50			
(A) Orange tanks	150	650	_____
(B) Black tanks	5	20	_____
(C) Silver tanks	3	12	_____
625 Gulf, tank car, 1951	4	14	_____
625G Gulf, tank car, 1951-53	3	10	_____
627 AF Lines, flatcar, 1950	5	20	_____
627 C & NWRY, flatcar, mv, 1946-50	5	18	_____
(628) C & NWRY, flatcar, 1946-53	5	20	_____
629 MP, stock car, mv, 1946-53	5	12	_____
630 Reading, caboose, mv, 1946-53	3	10	_____
630 American Flyer, caboose, 1952	10	40	_____

	Good	Exc	Cond / $
630 AF Lines, caboose, 1952 (U)	4	15	
631 T & P, gondola, 1946-53			
(A) Green unpainted	2	6	
(B) 1948 (U), dark gray unpainted	60	250	
(C) 1952 (U), red-painted	20	90	
(D) 1946-52, green-painted	3	10	
(632) Virginian, hopper, 1946	20	80	
632 LNE, hopper, 1946-53			
(A) Gray plastic	2	8	
(B) 1946, black plastic	4	15	
(C) Gray-painted die-cast	25	95	
(D) White plastic	12	50	
(E) Painted body	4	15	
633 B & O, mv, 1946-52			
Boxcars	7	15	
Reefers			
(A) Red, 1952 (U)	20	90	
(B) Brown, 1952 (U)	25	100	
633F G. Fox & Co., boxcar, 1947 (U)*	NRS	NRS	
634 C & NWRY, floodlight, mv, 1946-49, 1953	5	25	
635 C & NWRY, crane, 1946-48	10	35	
(635) C & NWRY, crane, 1948-49			
(A) Yellow cab	10	30	
(B) Red cab	50	250	
636 Erie, flatcar, 1948-53			
(A) Die-cast metal frame	10	30	
(B) 1953 (U), pressed-wood frame	70	300	
637 MKT, boxcar, mv, 1949-53*	6	20	
638 AF, caboose, mv, 1950-52	3	8	
638 AFL, caboose, 1953	3	8	
639 American Flyer, 1949-52			
Boxcars 1949-52, mv	4	8	
Reefers			
(A) Yellow body	4	10	
(B) Unpainted cream plastic body	30	130	
640 American Flyer, hopper, 1949-53			
(A) White lettering	2	8	
(B) Black lettering	2	8	
(C) White plastic body w/black lett	10	50	
640 Wabash, hopper, 1953	5	22	
641 American Flyer, gondola, 1949-52			
(A) Red-painted or unpainted plastic	5	15	
(B) 1951 (U), gray unpainted	50	200	
641 Frisco, gondola, 1953	5	18	
642 Seaboard, boxcar, 1953	6	15	

	Good	Exc	Cond / $
642 American Flyer, 1951-52			
Boxcars 1951-52	4	8	______
Reefers 1952 (U)			
(A) Red- or brown-painted body	4	12	______
(B) Brown-painted w/Type B trucks	4	8	______
(643) AF Circus, flatcar, 1950-53*			
(A) With two cages, truck tractor	50	200	______
(A) With car only	5	20	______
644 American Flyer, crane, 1950-53			
(A) Black cab, black-ptd. gray boom	10	50	______
(B) 1950, red cab, black boom	20	125	______
(C) 1950, red cab, green boom	10	55	______
(D) 1950-51, brown-painted cab, green boom	15	60	______
645 AF, work and boom car, 1950	7	25	______
645A AFL, work and boom car, 1951-53	6	25	______
(646) Erie, floodlight, 1950-53			
(A) 1950, green-painted die-cast gen.	40	175	______
(B) Other variations	10	30	______
647 NP, reefer, 1952-53	10	35	______
648 American Flyer, flatcar, 1952-54	10	30	______
(649) AF Circus, coach, mv, 1950-52	20	75	______
650 New Haven, Pullman, mv, 1946-53			
(A) Red or green with plastic frame	15	45	______
(B) Red or green with die-cast frame	10	45	______
(C) Red or green w/sheet metal frame	10	45	______
651 New Haven, baggage, mv, 1946-53			
(A) Red or green with plastic frame	15	35	______
(B) Red or green with die-cast frame	10	45	______
(C) Red or green w/sheet metal frame	10	45	______
652 Pullman, mv, 1946-53			
(A) Red or green, short trucks	20	85	______
(B) Red or green, long trucks	NRS	150	______
(C) Red or green, "Pikes Peak"	20	95	______
653 Pullman, mv, 1946-53			
(A) Red or green, long trucks	NRS	150	______
(B) Red or green, short trucks	20	85	______
654 Pullman, observation, mv, 1946-53			
(A) Red or green, long trucks	20	95	______
(B) Red or green, short trucks	20	85	______
655 Silver Bullet, coach, 1953			
(A) Chrome	15	75	______
(B) Satin aluminum	15	75	______
655 AF Lines, coach, 1953			
(A) Red	20	45	______
(B) Green	20	45	______

	Good	Exc	Cond / $
660 AFL, combination, 1950-52			
(A) Extruded aluminum shell	20	40	
(B) Chrome-finished, plastic shell	20	60	
661 AFL, coach, 1950-52			
(A) Extruded aluminum shell	20	40	
(B) Chrome-finished, plastic shell	20	60	
(C) Satin silver	NRS	NRS	
662 AFL, vista dome, 1950-52			
(A) Extruded aluminum shell	20	40	
(B) Chrome-finished, plastic shell	20	60	
663 AFL, observation, 1950-52	20	40	
668 Manual switch, LH, 1953-55	4	8	
669 Manual switch, RH, 1953-55	4	8	
670 Track trip, 1955-56	1	4	
678 RC switch, LH, 1953-56	7	15	
679 RC switch, RH, 1953-56	7	15	
680 Curve track, 1946-48	.20	.50	
681 Straight track, 1946-48	.20	.50	
688 RC switches, pair, 1946-48	20	50	
690 Track terminal, 1946-56	.25	.75	
691 Steel pins, 1946-48	.50	1	
692 Fiber pins, 1946-48	.25	.75	
693 Track locks, 1948-56	.02	.07	
694 Coupler, truck, wheels, axles, 46-53	3	8	
695 Track trip, 1946	NRS	NRS	
695 Reverse loop relay, 1955-56	10	45	
696 Track trip, 1955-57	4	20	
697 Track trip, 1950-54	2	5	
698 Reverse loop kit, 1949-50, 1952-54	5	40	
700 Straight track, 1946-56	.15	.35	
701 ½ straight track, 1946-56	.15	.35	
702 Curve track, 1946-56	.15	.35	
703 ½ curve track, 1946-56	.10	.20	
704 Manual uncoupler, 1952-56	.25	.75	
705 RC uncoupler, 1946-47	1	3	
706 RC uncoupler, 1948-56	.35	1	
707 Track terminal, 1946-59	.15	.35	
708 Air chime whistle control, 1951-56	2	6	
709 Lockout eliminator, 1950-55	1	4	
710 Steam whistle control, 1955-56	4	20	
710 Automatic track section, 1946-47	.50	1.50	
711 Mail pickup, 1946-47	NRS	NRS	
712 Special rail section, 1947-56	.50	1	
713 Special rail section with mail bag hook, 1947-56	7	15	
714 Log unloading car, flatcar, 1951-54	12	40	
715 AF Lines, flatcar, mv, 1946-54	15	50	

	Good	Exc	Cond / $
716 AF Lines, hopper, 1946-51	7	30	______
717 AF Lines, flatcar, 1946-52	8	40	______
718 NH, mail pickup, mv, 1946-54	20	45	______
719 CB & Q, hopper dump car, 1950-54			
(A) Maroon-painted	15	70	______
(B) Red plastic	20	85	______
720 RC switches, 1946-49	10	35	______
720A RC switches, 1950-56	10	35	______
722 Manual switches, 1946-51	5	15	______
722A Manual switches, 1952-56	5	15	______
725 Crossing, 1946-56	1	4	______
726 Straight rubber roadbed, 1950-56	.50	1.50	______
727 Curved rubber roadbed, 1950-56	.50	1.50	______
728 Re-railer, 1956	1	5	______
730 Bumper, 1946-56			
(A) Green plastic	2	10	______
(B) 1951, red	20	75	______
731 Pike planning kit, 1952-56	8	15	______
732 AF, operating baggage car, 1951-54			
(A) Green unpainted plastic shell	20	50	______
(B) Green-painted plastic shell	20	75	______
(C) Unpainted red plastic shell	20	50	______
734 AF, operating boxcar, 1950-54	10	35	______
735 NH, animated station coach, 52-54	20	65	______
736 MP, stock car, 1950-54	7	25	______
(740) AFL, motorized unit, handcar			
(A) 1952, no decals, no vent holes	15	75	______
(B) With shield decal	10	50	______
741 AFL, handcar and shed, motorized unit, 1953	40	170	______
(742) AFL, handcar, motorized unit, 1955-56			
(A) Decal with stripes	35	150	______
(B) Decal without stripes	35	150	______
743 See (23)743			
747 Cardboard trestle set (U)	4	10	______
748 Overhead foot bridge, 1951-52	5	18	______
748 Girder, trestle, tower bridge, 1958 (U)	20	40	______
749 Street lamp set, 1950-52	5	15	______
750 Trestle bridge, 1946-56	10	35	______
751 Log loader, 1946-50	30	125	______
751A Log loader, 1952-53	30	145	______
752 Seaboard coaler, 1946-50	50	125	______
752A Seaboard coaler, 1951-52	50	135	______
753 Single trestle bridge, 1952	12	50	______
753 Mountain, tunnel, and passenger set, 1960 (U)	7	20	______

	Good	Exc	Cond / $
754 Double trestle bridge, 1950-52	17	50	
755 Talking station, 1948-50			
(A) Green roof	15	55	
(B) Blue roof	25	65	
758 Sam the Semaphore Man, 1949	12	40	
758A Sam the Semaphore Man, 1950-56	15	45	
759 Bell danger signal, mv, 1953-56	10	25	
760 Highway flasher, 1949-56	6	15	
761 Semaphore, 1949-56	10	30	
762 Two in one whistle, 1949-50	7	50	
763 Mountain set, 1949-50	25	175	
764 Express office, 1950-51	25	80	
766 Animated station, 1952-54	35	100	
K766 Animated station, 1953-55	35	100	
767 Roadside diner, 1950-54	10	50	
768 Oil supply depot, 1950-53			
(A) "Shell"	20	75	
(B) "Gulf"	25	90	
769 Aircraft beacon, 1950	6	25	
769A Aircraft beacon, 1951-56	6	20	
770 Baggage platform, 1950-52	22	60	
770 Girder trestle set, 1960 (U)	8	15	
771 Operating stockyard, 1950-54	18	80	
K771 Stockyard and car, 1953-56	20	80	
772 Water tower, 1950-56			
(A) "AMERICAN FLYER"	10	35	
(B) "THE COLBER CORPORATION"	10	35	
(C) Checkerboard	15	75	
773 Oil derrick, 1950-52			
(A) 1950, "American Flyer"	10	50	
(B) Colber plates	10	40	
774 Floodlight tower, mv, 1951-56	10	35	
775 Baggage platform, 1953-55	20	60	
K775 Baggage platform, KC, 1953-55	25	70	
778 Street lamp set, 1953-56	5	20	
779 Oil drum loader, 1955-56	30	85	
780 Trestle set, 1953-56	2	5	
781 Abutment set, 1953	15	40	
782 Abutment set, 1953	5	30	
783 Hi-trestle sections, 1953-56	5	15	
784 Hump set, 1955	NRS	NRS	
785 Coal loader, 1955-56	65	135	
787 Log loader, 1955-56	40	125	
788 Suburban station, 1956	7	40	
789 Sta. & baggage smasher, 1956-57	40	130	
790 Trainorama, 1953 (U)	20	100	

		Good	Exc	Cond / $
792	Terminal, 1954-56	30	120	_____
793	Union Station, 1955-56	15	75	_____
794	Union Station, 1954	25	80	_____
795	Union Station and terminal, 1954	65	350	_____
799	Talking station, 1954-56	20	90	_____
801	B & O, hopper, 1956-57	3	15	_____
802	IC, reefer, 1956-57*	5	14	_____
803	ATSF, boxcar, 1956-57	10	20	_____
804	N & W, gondola, 1956-57	3	8	_____
805	Pennsylvania, gondola, 1956-57			
	(A) Tuscan unpainted plastic	3	8	_____
	(B) Tuscan-painted black plastic	3	8	_____
806	AFL, caboose, 1956-57	4	10	_____
807	Rio Grande, boxcar, 1957			
	(A) Non-opening door	7	20	_____
	(B) Opening door	NRS	NRS	_____
812	See (21)812			
900	NP, combination, 1956-57*	100	275	_____
901	NP, coach, 1956-57*	100	275	_____
902	NP, vista dome, 1956-57*	100	275	_____
903	NP, observation, 1956-57*	100	275	_____
904	AFL, caboose, 1956	3	8	_____
905	AF Lines, flatcar, 1954			
	(A) Gray-painted body	8	35	_____
	(B) Blue-painted body	8	35	_____
906	AF Lines, crane, 1954	10	40	_____
907	AFL, work and boom car, 1954	10	40	_____
909	AF Lines, flatcar, 1954			
	(A) Gray-painted body	8	35	_____
	(B) Blue-painted body	8	35	_____
910	Gilbert Chemical, tank car, 1954*	50	200	_____
911	C & O, gondola, 1955-57			
	(A) Silver pipes	5	28	_____
	(B) Brown plastic pipes	25	100	_____
912	Koppers, tank car, 1955-56	10	50	_____
913	GN, boxcar, 1953-58			
	(A) Decal	10	25	_____
	(B) Stamped	10	25	_____
914	AF Lines, flatcar, 1953-57	10	45	_____
915	AF Lines, flatcar, mv, 1953-57	15	60	_____
916	D & H, gondola, 1955-56	5	20	_____
918	AFL, mail car, 1953-58			
	(A) "American Flyer Lines"	25	60	_____
	(B) "New Haven"	25	70	_____
919	CB & Q, hopper dump car, 1953-56	15	65	_____
920	Southern, gondola, 1953-56	5	22	_____
921	CB & Q, hopper, 1953-56	5	25	_____

	Good	Exc	Cond / $
922 GAEX, boxcar, 1953-57*			
(A) Decal	10	30	____
(B) Stamped	10	30	____
923 IC, reefer, 1954-55*	7	18	____
924 CRP, hopper, 1953-56	5	20	____
925 Gulf, tank car, 1952-56	4	15	____
926 Gulf, tank car, 1955-56	10	45	____
928 New Haven, flatcar, 1954	8	30	____
(928) C & NWRY, flatcar, 1953-54			
(A) Pressed-wood base	10	55	____
(B) Die-cast base	8	20	____
928 New Haven, flatcar, 1956-57	5	20	____
929 MP, stock car, 1953-56	6	20	____
930 American Flyer, caboose, 1952 (U)			
(A) Red	9	40	____
(B) Tuscan	6	25	____
930 American Flyer Lines, caboose, 1953-57			
(A) Brown	3	15	____
(B) Tuscan	10	35	____
931 T & P, gondola, 1953-55	3	10	____
933 B & O, boxcar, 1953-54	10	35	____
934 American Flyer Lines, caboose (U)	10	35	____
934 C & NWRY, floodlight, 1953-54	5	25	____
934 SP, floodlight, 1954 (U)	10	40	____
935 AFL, caboose, 1957	15	70	____
936 Erie, flatcar, 1953-56	8	30	____
936 Pennsylvania, flatcar, 1953-57	25	100	____
937 MKT, boxcar, 1953-58*			
(A) All yellow	8	30	____
(B) Yellow and brown	8	30	____
938 AFL, caboose, 1954-55	2	6	____
940 Wabash, hopper, 1953-56	5	20	____
941 Frisco Lines, gondola, 1953-56	3	12	____
942 Seaboard, boxcar, 1954			
(A) White body	7	20	____
(B) Black body	7	20	____
944 American Flyer, crane, 1952-56	10	50	____
945 AFL, work and boom car, 1953-57	10	30	____
(946) Erie, floodlight, mv, 1953-56	10	35	____
947 NP, reefer, 1953-58	10	35	____
948 AF Lines, flatcar, 1953-56	7	25	____
951 AF Lines, baggage, mv, 1953-57			
(A) Red	15	40	____
(B) Green	20	45	____
952 AF Lines, Pullman, 1953-58			
(A) W/o silhouettes, maroon or green	40	175	____
(B) With silhouettes, maroon	50	200	____

	Good	Exc	Cond / $
953 AF Lines, combination, 1953-58			
(A) W/o silhouettes, maroon or green	35	150	_____
(B) With silhouettes, maroon	50	200	_____
954 AF Lines, observation, 1953-56			
(A) W/o silhouettes, maroon or green	35	150	_____
(B) With silhouettes, maroon	50	200	_____
955 AF Lines, coach, 1954			
(A) Satin silver-painted	15	75	_____
(B) Green-painted	15	75	_____
(C) Tuscan-painted, w/silhouettes and "955"	15	75	_____
(D) Tuscan-painted, w/silhouettes and white-outlined windows	25	100	_____
956 Monon, flatcar, 1956	15	65	_____
957 Erie, operating boxcar, 1957 (U)	20	95	_____
958 Mobilgas, tank car, 1957 (U)	15	70	_____
960 AFL, Columbus, combination, 1953-56			
(A) No color band	25	100	_____
(B) Blue, green, or red band	25	100	_____
(C) Chestnut band	50	200	_____
(D) Orange band	35	150	_____
961 AFL, Jefferson, Pullman, 1953-58			
(A) No color band	25	100	_____
(B) Blue band		Not Produced	
(C) Green or red band	25	100	_____
(D) Chestnut band	60	250	_____
(D) Orange band	35	150	_____
962 AFL, Hamilton, vista dome, 1953-58			
(A) No color band	25	100	_____
(B) Blue, green, or red band	25	100	_____
(C) Chestnut band	60	250	_____
(D) Orange band	35	150	_____
963 AFL, Washington, passenger car, 1953-58			
(A) No color band	25	100	_____
(B) Blue, green, or red band	25	100	_____
(C) Chestnut band	60	250	_____
(D) Orange band	35	150	_____
969 Rocket Launcher, flatcar, 1957 (U)	15	60	_____
970 Seaboard, oper. boxcar, 1956-57	15	50	_____
971 Southern Pacific, flatcar, 1956-57	30	120	_____
973 Gilbert oper. milk car, 1956-57	30	100	_____
974 AF Lines, oper. boxcar, 1953-54	20	65	_____
974 Erie, operating boxcar, 1955	30	100	_____
975 AFL, operating coach, 1955	15	65	_____
976 MP, operating cattle car, 1953-62	10	40	_____
977 AFL, caboose, 1955-57	9	35	_____

	Good	Exc	Cond / $
978 AFL, Grand Canyon, observation, 1956-58	60	250	____
979 AFL, caboose, 1957	15	80	____
980 B & O, boxcar, 1956-57	25	100	____
981 Central of Georgia, boxcar, 1956			
(A) Shiny black paint	30	85	____
(B) Dull black paint	35	125	____
982 BAR, boxcar, 1956-57	20	70	____
983 MP, boxcar, 1956-57	20	100	____
984 New Haven, boxcar, 1956-57	20	65	____
985 BM, boxcar, 1957	20	75	____
988 ART Co., reefer, 1956	15	70	____
989 Northwestern, reefer, 1956-58	30	125	____
994 UP, stock car, 1957	25	150	____
C1001 WSX, boxcar, 1962 (U)*	NRS	NRS	____
L2001 Game Train, 4-4-0, 1963	5	20	____
L2002 Burlington Route or Erie, 4-4-0, 1963 (U)			
(A) "Burlington Route"	55	225	____
(B) "Erie"	50	210	____
L-2004 Rio Grande, EMD F-9, 1962	60	180	____
C-2009 Texas & Pacific, gondola, 1962-64			
(A) Dark green	NRS	NRS	____
(B) Light green	3	10	____
5300T Miners work train, motorized unit, 1953-54*	80	300	____
7210 See (636), (646), 936, (946), or (24529)			
1-1024 A Trestle set, 1952 (U)	10	45	____
21004 PRR, 0-6-0, switcher, 1957 (U)	75	300	____
21005 PRR, 0-6-0, switcher, 1957-58	100	400	____
(21030) See 307			
(21034) See 303			
(21044) See 313			
(21058) See 326			
21084 CNW, 4-6-2, Pacific, 1957 (U)	30	120	____
21085 CNW or CMStP & P or RL, 4-6-2, Pacific, 1958-65	15	60	____
(210)88 FY & P, 4-4-0, Franklin, 59-60	20	95	____
(21089) FY & PRR, 4-4-0, Wash., 60-61	65	250	____
21095 NYNH & H, 4-6-2, Pacific, 1957	NRS	NRS	____
21099 NYNH & H, 4-6-2, Pacific, 1958	75	250	____
21100 RL, 4-4-2, Atlantic, 1957 (U)	7	25	____
21105 RL, 4-4-2, Atlantic, 1957-58	7	25	____
21106 RL, 4-4-2, Atlantic, 1959 (U)	40	160	____
21107 RL or PRR or BN, 4-4-2, Atlantic, 1964-65 (U)	10	30	____
21115 PRR, 4-6-2, Pacific, 1958	175	700	____

	Good	Exc	Cond / $
21129 NYC, 4-6-4, Hudson, 1958	250	1000	_____
21130 NYC, 4-6-4, Hudson, 1959-60	75	300	_____
21139 UP, 4-8-4, Northern, 1958-59	175	700	_____
21140 UP, 4-8-4, Northern, 1960	325	1350	_____
21145 NKP, 0-8-0, switcher, 1958	125	500	_____
21155 Steam, 0-6-0, switcher, 1958	75	260	_____
21156 Steam, 0-6-0, switcher, 1959	60	230	_____
21158 Steam, 0-6-0, switcher, 1960 (U)	30	115	_____
21160 RL, 4-4-2, Atlantic, 1958-60 (U)	10	20	_____
21161 RL, 4-4-2, Atlantic, 1960 (U)			
(A) "American Flyer Lines"	7	20	_____
(B) "Prestone Car Care Express"	50	200	_____
21165 Erie or CMStP & P, 4-4-0, 1961-62, 1965-66 (U)	7	15	_____
21166 Burlington Route, 4-4-0, 1963-64, 1965-66 (U)			
(A) White letters	5	15	_____
(B) Black letters	50	200	_____
21168 Southern, 4-4-0, 1961-63	10	40	_____
21205/21205-1 BM, twin EMD F-9s, 1961 (U), 1962	75	170	_____
21206/21206-1 SF, twin EMD F-9s, 1962 (U)	80	200	_____
21207/21207-1 GN, twin EMD F-9s, 1963-64	90	225	_____
21210 Burlington, EMD F-9, 1961	40	170	_____
21215/21215-1 UP, EMD F-9, 1961-62	70	220	_____
21215/21216 UP, twin EMD F-9s, 1961	NRS	NRS	_____
(21)234 C & O, GP-7, 1960-61			
(A) Long steps	140	450	_____
(B) Short steps	160	500	_____
21551 NP, PA, 1958	140	350	_____
(21552/21556) See 490/492			
(21560) See 497			
21561 New Haven, PA, 1957-58			
(A) Plastic steps	100	300	_____
(B) One-rivet metal steps	125	350	_____
(21570) See 499			
(21571) See 499			
21573 NH, GE electric, 1958-59	150	500	_____
21720 Santa Fe, PB, 1958 (U)	350	1200	_____
(21800) See 355			
21801 CNW, Baldwin, 1957-58	50	140	_____
21801-1 CNW, Baldwin, 1958 (U)	60	200	_____
21808 CNW, Baldwin, 1958 (U)	40	125	_____

	Good	Exc	Cond / $
(21)812 T & P, Baldwin, 1959-60	70	190	
21813 MStL, Baldwin, 1958 (U)	200	600	
(21820) See 372			
(21821) See 372			
21831 Texas & Pacific, GP-7, 1958			
(A) "American Flyer Lines"	150	425	
(B) "Texas & Pacific"	180	550	
21910/21910-1/21910-2 SF, PA/PB/PA, 1957-58	275	900	
21918/21918-1 Seaboard, Baldwin, 1958	200	800	
21920/21920-1 MP, PA/PA, 1958*	325	1100	
21920 MP, PA, 1963-64	150	600	
21922/21922-1 MP, PA/PA, 1959	300	1000	
21925/21925-1 UP, PA/PA, 1959-60*	300	1200	
21927 Santa Fe, PA, 1960-62	125	300	
22004 40-watt transformer, 1959-64	1	3	
22006 25-watt transformer, 1963	2	8	
22020 50-watt transformer, 1957-64	2	6	
22030 100-watt transformer, 1957-64	2	10	
22033 25-watt transformer, 1965	1	3	
22034 110-watt transformer, 1965	2	9	
22035 175-watt transformer, 1957-64	15	55	
22040 110-watt transformer, 1957-58	6	20	
22050 175-watt transformer, 1957-58	10	30	
22060 175-watt transformer, 1957-58	10	35	
22080 300-watt transformer, 1957-58	20	55	
22090 350-watt transformer, 1959-64	20	70	
23021 Imitation grass, 1957-59	4	15	
23022 Scenery gravel, 1957-59	2	10	
23023 Imitation coal, 1957-59	2	10	
23024 Rainbow wire, 1957-64	2	10	
23025 Smoke cartridges, 1957-59	3	5	
23026 Service kit, 1959-64	3	15	
23027 Track cleaning fluid, 1957-59	1	3	
23028 Smoke fluid dispenser, 1960-64	1	3	
23032 Equipment kit, 1960-61	10	25	
23036 Money saver kit, 1960, 62, 64	10	30	
23040 Mountain, tunnel, and passenger set, 1958	NRS	NRS	
23249 Tunnel, 1957-64	9	30	
23320 AF traffic master, 1960	NRS	NRS	
23561 Billboard horn, 1957-59	7	30	
23568 Whistling billboard, 1957-64	7	25	
23571 Truss bridge, 1957-64	3	12	
23581 Girder bridge, 1957-64	3	15	

		Good	Exc	Cond / $
23586	Wayside station, 1957-59	15	40	_____
23589	Pass. and freight sta., 1959 (U)	15	40	_____
23590	Control tower, 1957-59	15	50	_____
23596	Water tank, 1957-58	15	55	_____
23598	Talking station record, 1957-59	3	15	_____
23599	Talking station record, 1957	6	30	_____
23600	Crossing gate with bell, 1957-58	10	35	_____
23601	Crossing gate, 1959-62	5	30	_____
23602	Crossing gate, 1963-64	15	40	_____
(23)743	Track maintenance car	NRS	NRS	_____
23743	Track maintenance car, 1960-64	50	150	_____
23750	Trestle bridge, 1957-61	15	35	_____
23758	Sam the Semaphore Man, 1957	12	40	_____
23759	Bell danger signal, 1956-60	10	30	_____
23760	Highway flasher, 1957-60	6	15	_____
23761	Semaphore, 1957-60	8	30	_____
23763	Bell danger signal, 1961-64	6	25	_____
23764	Flasher signal, 1961-64	6	20	_____
23769	Aircraft beacon, 1957-64	6	25	_____
23771	Stockyard and car, 1957-61	18	80	_____
23772	Water tower, 1957-64	10	75	_____
23774	Floodlight tower, 1957-64	10	35	_____
23778	Street lamp set, 1957-64	5	20	_____
23779	Oil drum loader, 1957-61	30	85	_____
23780	Gabe the Lamplighter, 1958-59			
	(A) Plastic shed	NRS	NRS	_____
	(B) Metal shed	100	550	_____
23785	Coal loader, 1957-60	65	135	_____
23786	Talking station, 1957-59	40	80	_____
23787	Log loader, 1957-60	40	125	_____
23788	Suburban station, 1957-64	10	40	_____
23789	Station and baggage smasher, 1958-59	40	130	_____
23791	Cow-on-track, 1957-59	20	55	_____
23796	Sawmill, 1957-64	60	150	_____
23830	Piggy back unloader, 1959-60	15	60	_____
24003	ATSF, boxcar, 1958	15	45	_____
24016	MKT, boxcar, 1958	150	600	_____
24019	Seaboard, boxcar, 1958 (U)	15	35	_____
24023	B & O, boxcar, 1958-59	30	150	_____
24026	C of G, boxcar, 1958	30	125	_____
24029	BAR, boxcar, 1957-60	35	125	_____
24030	MKT, boxcar, 1960 (U)			
	(A) Unpainted yellow plastic	10	20	_____
	(B) Yellow-painted plastic	NRS	NRS	_____
24033	MP, boxcar, 1958	40	110	_____

	Good	Exc	Cond / $
24036 New Haven, boxcar, 1958	20	75	
24039 Rio Grande, boxcar, 1959	10	30	
24043 BM, boxcar, 1958-60	25	80	
24045 MEC, boxcar	NRS	NRS	
24047 GN, boxcar, 1959	50	200	
24048 MStL, boxcar, 1959-62	40	100	
24052 UFGE, boxcar, 1961	5	15	
24054 Santa Fe, boxcar, 1962-64, 1966			
(A) 1962-64, red-painted plastic	20	40	
(B) 1966, red unpainted plastic	10	40	
(C) Red unpainted, knuckle couplers	20	45	
(240)55 The Gold Belt Line, boxcar, 1960-61			
(A) With sticker	12	45	
(B) Without sticker	12	45	
24056 BM, boxcar, 1961			
(A) Blue-painted black plastic	25	120	
(B) Unpainted blue plastic	25	110	
24057 Mounds, boxcar, 1962	5	10	
24058 Post, boxcar, 1963-64			
(A) White shell	5	10	
(B) Cream-colored plastic with "marble" finish	6	20	
24059 BM, boxcar, 1963	40	160	
24060 MStL, boxcar, 1963-64	30	110	
24065 NYC, boxcar, 1960-64			
(A) Knuckle couplers	30	75	
(B) Pike Master couplers	30	60	
24065 NYC, reefer	NRS	NRS	
24066 L & N, boxcar, 1960			
(A) Black plastic body	50	150	
(B) White shell	55	165	
(24067) Keystone Line, boxcar, 1960 (U)*	NRS	NRS	
24068 Planters Peanuts, boxcar, 1961 (U)*	NRS	NRS	
(24072) See 929			
24076 UP, stock car, mv, 1957-60			
(A) With knuckle couplers	12	45	
(B) With Pike Master couplers	12	45	
24077 Northern Pacific, stock car, 1959-62			
(A) Knuckle couplers	60	160	
(B) Pike Master couplers	50	150	
24103 N & W, gondola, 1958, 1963-64			
(A) Black plastic	4	15	
(B) Brown plastic	QE	QE	
24106 Pennsylvania, gondola, 1960 (U)	3	12	
(24108) See 911			

	Good	Exc	Cond / $
24109 C & O, gondola, 1957-60			
(A) Silver plastic or cardboard pipes	6	25	______
(B) Brown plastic pipes	25	100	______
(C) Orange cardboard pipes	12	50	______
24110 Pennsylvania, gondola, 1959 (U)	3	12	______
24113 D & H, gondola, 1957-59	10	40	______
24116 Southern, gondola, 1957-60	10	45	______
24120 T & P, gondola, 1960	10	45	______
(24122) See 941			
24124 Boston and Maine, gondola, 1963-64			
(A) Unpainted blue	3	12	______
(B) Dark blue-painted	15	75	______
24125 Bethlehem Steel, gondola, 1960-64			
(A) Gray-painted	20	85	______
(B) Unpainted gray	2	8	______
24126 Frisco, gondola, 1961	25	100	______
24127 Monon, gondola, 1961-65			
(A) Knuckle couplers	2	10	______
(B) Pike Master couplers	2	10	______
(24130) Pennsylvania, gondola, 1960 (U)			
(A) Pike Master couplers	5	20	______
(B) Fixed or operating knuckles	2	8	______
24203 B & O, hopper, 1958, 1963-64			
(A) 1958, unpainted trucks	5	20	______
(B) 1958, black-painted trucks	NRS	NRS	______
(C) 1963-64, PM trucks and couplers	10	45	______
(24205) See 921			
24206 CB & Q, hopper, 1958	15	65	______
(24208) See 924			
24209 CRP, hopper, 1957-60	12	50	______
24213 Wabash, hopper, 1958-60	10	35	______
24216 Union Pacific, hopper, 1958-60	15	65	______
24219 West. Maryland, hopper, 1958-59	25	110	______
24221 C & EI, hopper, 1959-60	30	125	______
24222 Domino Sugars, hopper, 1963-64*	75	350	______
24225 Santa Fe, hopper, 1960-65	10	40	______
24230 Peabody, hopper, 1961-64			
(A) Knuckle couplers	15	75	______
(B) Pike Master couplers	10	40	______
24309 Gulf, tank car, 1957-58	5	25	______
24310 Gulf, tank car, 1958-60	5	20	______
24313 Gulf, tank car, 1957-60	15	60	______
24316 Mobilgas, tank car, 1957-61, 1965-66			
(A) Knuckle couplers	8	35	______
(B) Pike Master couplers	5	20	______
24319 PRR Salt, tank car, 1958*	125	500	______

		Good	Exc	Cond / $
24320	Deep Rock, tank car, 1960	75	300	
24321	Deep Rock, tank car, 1959	15	60	
24322	Gulf, tank car, 1959	15	70	
24323	Baker's Chocolate, tank car, 1959-60*			
	(A) White with white ends	500	2000	
	(B) White with gray-painted ends	60	250	
24324	Hooker, tank car, 1959-60	15	70	
24325	Gulf, tank car, 1960			
	(A) Type II plastic frame	4	15	
	(B) Type III plastic frame	10	30	
24328	Shell, tank car, 1962-66	4	15	
24329	Hooker, tank car, 1964-65	7	30	
(24329)	Hooker, tank car, 1961-65	7	30	
24330	Baker's Chocolate, tank car, 1961-62	10	50	
24403	IC, reefer, (U)*	7	18	
24409	NP, reefer, 1958	300	1200	
24413	ART Co., reefer, 1957-60	30	120	
24416	NW, reefer, 1958	600	2000	
24419	CN, reefer, 1958-59	50	225	
(24420)	Simmons, reefer, 1958* (U)	NRS	1200	
24422	Great Northern, 1963-65, 1966 (U)			
	Boxcars	35	120	
	Reefers			
	(A) Unpainted green plastic, non-opening door	4	12	
	(B) Unpainted green plastic, opening door	20	90	
	(C) Green-painted plastic, non-opening door	40	175	
24425	BAR, reefer, 1960	80	400	
24426	Rath Packing Co., reefer, 1960-61	80	400	
24516	New Haven, flatcar, 1957-59	7	25	
24519	Pennsylvania, flatcar, 1958	250	1000	
(24522)	See 944			
(24525)	See 945			
(24529)	Erie, floodlight, 1957-58	10	35	
24533	AF Lines, flatcar, 1958-66	7	25	
24536	Monon, flatcar, 1958	250	1000	
24537	New Haven, flatcar, 1958 (U)	10	45	
24539	New Haven, flatcar, 1958-59, 1963-64			
	(A) 1958-59, silver plastic or cardboard pipes	10	35	
	(B) 1963-64, orange cardboard pipes	12	45	
24540	New Haven, flatcar, 1960 (U)	45	180	
24543	AF Lines, crane, 1958	10	35	

	Good	Exc	Cond / $
24546 AFL, work and boom car, 58-64	10	30	
24547 Erie, floodlight, 1958	NRS	NRS	
24549 Erie, floodlight, 1958-66			
(A) Yellow generator, knuckle couplers	10	25	
(B) Red generator	10	25	
(C) Yellow generator, PM couplers	5	15	
24550 Monon, flatcar, 1959-64	15	70	
24553 Rocket Transport, flatcar, 58-60	20	85	
24556 Rock Island, flatcar, 1959	15	65	
24557 US Navy, flatcar, 1959-61	30	125	
24558 CP, flatcar, 1959-60	50	225	
24559 New Haven, flatcar, 1959 (U)	75	300	
24561 American Flyer Lines, crane, 1959-61			
(A) 1959, gray-painted frame, knuckle couplers	10	35	
(B) 1960-61, gray unpainted frame, Pike Master couplers	5	20	
24562 New York Central, flatcar, 1960	10	40	
(24564) New Haven, flatcar, 1960 (U)	10	40	
(245)65 FY & PRR, flatcar, 1960-61*	30	125	
24566 New Haven, flatcar, 1961-64			
(A) Black unpainted body	15	60	
(B) 1961, gray unpainted body	NRS	NRS	
(24566) Nat'l Car Co., flatcar, 1961-65	15	60	
24569 AF Lines, crane, 1962-66	7	18	
24572 US Navy, flatcar, 1961	40	150	
24574 US Air Force, flatcar, 1960-61			
(A) Knuckle couplers	30	150	
(B) Pike Master couplers	30	150	
24575 National Car Co., flatcar, 1960-66	7	35	
(24575) Unmarked, flatcar, 1966 (U)	7	35	
24577 Illinois Central, flatcar, 1960-61, 1963-64			
(A) Pike Master couplers	25	100	
(B) Knuckle couplers	25	110	
24578 New Haven, flatcar, 1962-63	75	300	
24579 Illinois Central, flatcar, 1960-61	30	125	
24603 AFL, caboose, 1958	2	10	
(24608) See 930			
24610 AFL, caboose	3	8	
24619 AFL, caboose, 1958	15	70	
24626 AFL, caboose, 1958	3	10	
24627 AFL, caboose, 1959-60	3	6	
24630 AFL, caboose	3	6	
24631 AFL, caboose, 1959-61	5	25	
24632 AFL, caboose	15	50	
24633 AFL, caboose, 1959-62	10	60	
24634 AFL, caboose, 1963-66	10	50	

	Good	Exc	Cond / $
24636 American Flyer Lines, caboose, 1961-66			
(A) Red	2	8	____
(B) Yellow	100	300	____
24638 AFL, caboose, 1962	10	60	____
(24702) See 901			
(24705) See 900			
(24708) See 902			
(24712) See 903			
(247)20 FY & PRR, coach, 1959-61	10	40	____
(247)30 FY & PRR, Overland Express, baggage, 1959-60	10	40	____
24733 AFL, Pikes Peak, coach, 1957	75	325	____
24739 AFL, Niagara Falls, combination, 1957	NRS	NRS	____
(247)40 Baggage Express, comb., 1960	10	40	____
(247)50 FY & PRR, comb., 1960-61	30	125	____
(24772) See 960			
24773 AFL, Columbus, combination, 1957-58, 1960-62	35	150	____
(24775) See 960			
24776 AFL, Columbus, combination, 1957, 1959			
(A) 1959, orange stripe	35	150	____
(B) 1957, red stripe	QE	QE	____
(24792) See 961			
24793 AFL, Jefferson, Pullman, 1957-58, 1960-62	35	150	____
24794 AFL, Jefferson, coach	NRS	NRS	____
(24795) See 961			
24796 AFL, Jefferson, Pullman, 1957, 1959			
(A) 1959, orange stripe	35	150	____
(B) 1957, red stripe	QE	QE	____
(24812) See 962			
24813 AFL, Hamilton, vista dome, 1957-58, 1960-62	35	150	____
24816 AFL, Hamilton, vista dome, 1957, 1959			
(A) 1957, red stripe	QE	QE	____
(B) 1959, orange stripe	35	150	____
(24816) See 963			
(24832) See 963			
24833 AFL, Washington, observation, 1957-58, 1960-62	35	150	____
(24835) See 963			
24836 AFL, Washington, observation			
(A) 1959, orange stripe	35	150	____
(B) 1957, red stripe	QE	QE	____
24837 UP, combination, 1959-60*	75	300	____
24838 UP, coach, 1959-60*	80	350	____

	Good	Exc	Cond / $
24839 UP, vista dome, 1959-60*	80	350	
24840 UP, observation, 1959-60*	75	300	
24843 NP, combination, 1958	60	250	
24846 NP, coach, 1958	60	250	
24849 NP, vista dome, 1958	60	250	
24853 NP, observation, 1958	60	250	
24856 (MP) Eagle Hill, combination, 1958, 1963-64*	110	450	
24859 (MP) Eagle Lake, coach, 1958, 1963-64*	125	500	
24863 (MP) Eagle Creek, coach, 1958, 1963-64*	125	500	
24866 (MP) Eagle Valley, observation, 1958, 1963-64*	110	450	
24867 American Flyer Lines, combination, 1958 (U), 1960 (U)	35	150	
24868 American Flyer Lines, observation, 1958 (U), 1960 (U)	35	150	
24869 American Flyer Lines, coach, 1958 (U), 1960 (U)	35	150	
25003 American Flyer, flatcar, 1957-60	50	200	
(25007) See 919			
(25012) See 970			
(25015) See 971			
25016 SP, flatcar, 1957-60	25	100	
25019 Operating milk car, 1957-60	40	125	
25025 CB & Q, dump car, 1958-60	40	160	
25031 AFL, caboose, 1958	NRS	NRS	
(25032) See 915			
(25033) See 915			
(25035) See 979			
25042 Erie, operating boxcar, 1958	40	150	
(25044) See 969			
25045 Rocket launcher, flatcar, 1957-60	15	65	
25046 Rocket launcher, flatcar, 1960	15	75	
25049 Rio Grande, boxcar, 1958-60	40	225	
25052 AFL, caboose, 1958	20	90	
(25056) USM and Rocket Launcher set, operating boxcar and flatcar, 1959	100	450	
25057 TNT, exploding boxcar, 1960	30	200	
25058 Southern Pacific, flatcar, 1961-64	30	120	
25059 Rocket launcher, flatcar, 1960-64	15	60	
25060 CB & Q, hopper dump car, 1961-64	50	200	
25061 TNT, exploding boxcar, 1961	35	250	
25062 Mine carrier, exploding boxcar, 1962-64	40	300	

		Good	Exc	Cond / $
25071	AF tie car, flatcar, 1961-64	7	30	____
25081	NYC, operating boxcar, 1961-64	10	35	____
25082	NH, operating boxcar, 1961-64	10	35	____
25515	USAF, flatcar, 1960-63	35	150	____
26101	Curve track panel, 1965-66	3	15	____
26121	Straight track panel, 1965-66	5	15	____
26122	Straight panel, 1965-66	7	35	____
26141	Right switch panel, 1965-66	7	15	____
26142	Left switch panel, 1965-66	7	15	____
26151	Crossover panel, 1965-66	7	12	____
26300	PM straight track, 1961-64	.10	.40	____
26301	PM straight track, 1961-64	.10	.40	____
26302	PM straight track, with uncoupler, 1961-64	.50	2	____
26310	PM curve track, 1961-64	.10	.35	____
26320	PM RH remote switch, 1961-64	3	9	____
26321	PM LH remote switch, 1961-64	3	9	____
26322	PM 90 degree crossing, 1961-64	1	3	____
26323	PM RH manual switch, 1961-64	2	6	____
26324	PM LH manual switch, 1961-64	2	6	____
26340	PM steel track pins, 1961-64	.40	.80	____
26341	PM insulating pins, 1961-64	.40	.80	____
26342	PM adapter pins, 1961-64	.30	.60	____
26343	PM track locks, 1961-64	.30	.60	____
26344	PM track terminal, 1961-64	.20	.40	____
26415	Track assortment, 1960, 1962	NRS	NRS	____
26425	Track assortment pack, 1960	6	12	____
26428	Accessory pack, 1958 (U)	NRS	NRS	____
26520	Knuckle coupler kit, 1957-64	1	5	____
26521	Knuckle coupler kit, 1957-58	6	25	____
26601	Fiber roadbed, 1959-62	.15	.50	____
26602	Fiber roadbed, 1959, 1961-62	.15	.50	____
26670	Track trip, 1957-58	2	6	____
26671	Track trip, 1959	2	6	____
26672	Track trip, 1960	2	6	____
26673	Track trip, 1961-64	2	6	____
26690	Track terminal, 1957-59	.50	2	____
26691	Steel pins, 1957-60, 1964	.30	.70	____
26692	Fiber pins, 1957-60, 1964	.20	.60	____
26693	Track locks, 1957-60, 1964	.50	1	____
26700	Straight track, 1957-64	.15	.40	____
26708	Horn control, 1957-58	2	6	____
26710	Straight track, 1957-64	.15	.35	____
26718	RC switch, LH, 1957	5	12	____
26719	RC switch, RH, 1957	5	12	____
26720	Curve track, 1957-64	.15	.35	____
26722	Curve track	NRS	NRS	____

		Good	Exc	Cond / $
26726	Rubber roadbed, half-straight section, 1958	.50	1.50	______
26727	Rubber roadbed, half curved, 58	.50	1.50	______
26730	Curve track, half section, 57-64	.15	.35	______
26739	Whistle control, 1957-58	.50	1.50	______
26742	RC switches, pair, 1957	15	35	______
26744	Manual switches, pair, 1957-58	9	15	______
26745	Railroad crossing, 1957-64	1	5	______
26746	Rubber roadbed, 1957-64	.50	1.50	______
26747	Rubber roadbed, 1957-64	.50	1.50	______
26748	Re-railer, 1957-64	1	5	______
26749	Bumper, 1957-60	1	10	______
26751	Pike planning kit, 1957-59	5	20	______
26752	RC uncoupler, 1957-58, 1960-61	1	2	______
26753	Manual uncoupler (U)	.50	1.00	______
26756	Bumper, 1961-64	1	10	______
26760	RC switches, pair, 1958-64	15	35	______
26761	RC switch, LH, 1958-64	7	17	______
26762	RC switch, RH, 1958-64	7	17	______
26770	Manual switches, pair, 1959-64	8	16	______
26781	Trestle set, 1957	10	20	______
26782	Trestle set, 1958-60	1	5	______
26783	Hi-trestles, 1957	5	20	______
26790	Trestle set, 1961-64	1	5	______
26810	Pow-R-Clips, 1960-64	.20	.40	______
27443	Lamps	1	3	______
27460	Lamp assortment, 1959, 1964	5	15	______

NUMERICAL LISTINGS
Lionel Production

		Mint Cond / $	
Southern Pacific Combine See (9500)			
Southern Pacific Coach See (9501)			
Southern Pacific Vista Dome See (9502)			
Southern Pacific Observation See (9503)			
Unlettered/unnumbered Diesel See (8154)			
390	Pennzoil, NASG, tank car, 1990	35	_____
491	NYC, reefer, 1991	CP	_____
591	Boraxo, hopper, 1991	CP	_____
0700	NASG, boxcar, 1981	60	_____
8000	See (4)8000		
8001	See (4)8001		
8002	See (4)8002		
8005	See (4)8005		
8007	See (4)8007		
8008	See (4)8008		
8009	See (4)8009		
8100/8101	Wabash, PA/PA, 1988	285	_____
8102/8103	C & O, PA/PA, 1989	285	_____
8106/8107	UP, PA/PA, 1990	300	_____
8112/8113	MP, PA/PA, 1991	CP	_____
8150/8151/8152	SP, PA/PB/PA, 1981	500	_____
8151	Southern Pacific, PB, 1982	150	_____
8153/(8154)/8155	B & O, PA/PB/PA, 81, 83	350	_____
(8154)	B & O, PB, 1981, 1983	80	_____
8251/8252/8253	Erie, PA/PB/PA, 1982	400	_____
8252	Erie, PB, 1982	125	_____
8308	See (4)8308		
8309	See (4)8309		
8310	See (4)8310		
8350	Boston and Maine, GP-7, 1983	350	_____
8458	Southern, GP-9, 1985	250	_____
8459	B & O, GP-20, 1985	275	_____
8460	B & O, GP-20, 1988	150	_____
8503	See (4)8503		
8551	Santa Fe, GP-20, 1986	250	_____
8552	New York Central, 1986	225	_____
8553	Santa Fe, 1988	150	_____
8706	See (4)8706		
8707	See (4)8707		
8805	See (4)8805		
8904	See (4)8904		
8905	See (4)8905		

		Mint Cond / $	
8906	See (4)8906		
8907	See (4)8907		
8908	See (4)8908		
8909	See (4)8909		
8910	See (4)8910		
8911	See (4)8911		
8912	See (4)8912		
8913	See (4)8913		
8914	See (4)8914		
8915	See (4)8915		
9000	B & O, flatcar, 1981, 1983	35	____
9001	See (4)9001		
9002	See (4)9002		
9002	Boston and Maine, flatcar, 1983	60	____
9004	Southern, flatcar, 1985	38	____
9005	New York Central, flatcar, 1986	25	____
9100	Gulf, tank car, 1979	50	____
9101	Union, tank car, 1980	25	____
9102	B & O, tank car, 1981, 1983	25	____
9104	Boston and Maine, tank car, 1983	65	____
9105	Southern, tank car, 1985	25	____
9106	New York Central, tank car, 1986	25	____
9200	B & O, hopper, 1979	50	____
9201	B & O, hopper, 1981, 1983	25	____
9203	Boston and Maine, hopper, 1983	60	____
9204	Southern, hopper, 1985	20	____
9205	Pennsylvania, hopper, 1985	35	____
9206	New York Central, hopper, 1985	25	____
9207	B & O, hopper, 1986	30	____
9208	ATSF, hopper, 1986	25	____
9209	New York Central, hopper, 1986	20	____
9300	Burlington, gondola, 1980	15	____
9301	B & O, gondola, 1982	25	____
9303	Southern, gondola, 1985	25	____
9304	New York Central, gondola, 1986	20	____
9400	B & O, caboose, 1980	20	____
9401	B & O, caboose, 1981, 1983	30	____
9402	BM, caboose, 1983	55	____
9403	Southern, caboose, 1985	30	____
9404	New York Central, caboose, 1986	30	____
9405	Santa Fe, caboose, 1986	30	____
(9500)	SP, combination, 1981	100	____
(9501)	SP, coach, 1981	150	____
(9502)	SP, vista dome, 1981	150	____
(9503)	SP, observation, 1981	100	____
9504	Erie, combination, 1982	60	____
9505	Erie, coach, 1982	120	____

		Mint Cond / $	
9506	Erie, vista dome, 1982	110	____
9507	Erie, observation, 1982	60	____
9700	AT & SF, boxcar, 1979	70	____
9701	The Rock, boxcar, 1980	33	____
9702	B & O, boxcar, 1981	40	____
9703	Boston and Maine, boxcar, 1983	75	____
9704	Southern, boxcar, 1985	30	____
9705	Pennsylvania, boxcar, 1985	35	____
9706	New York Central, boxcar, 1985	60	____
9707	Rail Box, boxcar, 1985	45	____
9708	Conrail, boxcar, 1985	35	____
9709	B & O, boxcar, 1986	30	____
9710	ATSF, boxcar, 1986	30	____
9711	Southern Pacific, boxcar, 1986	33	____
9712	Illinois Central Gulf, boxcar, 1986	30	____
9713	New York Central, boxcar, 1986	35	____
4-2300	Oil drum loader, 1985	95	____
4-2321	Operating sawmill, 1986-88	100	____
42597	See (635) or 635 (Gilbert Production)		
(4)8000	Southern Pacific, 1987	190	____
(4)8001	Illinois Central Gulf, 1987	190	____
(4)8002	SP, GP-9, 1988	150	____
(48003)	See 8553		
(48004)	See 8460		
(4)8005	Pennsylvania, GP-9, 1989	200	____
(4)8007	BN, GP-20, 1989	210	____
(4)8008	New Haven, GE electric, 1991	CP	____
(4)8009	AF, GP-7, 1991	CP	____
(4)8010	Milwaukee Road Electric, 1992	CP	____
(48100)	See 8100/8101		
(48102)	See 8102/8103		
(48106)	See 8106/8107		
(4)8117	Northern Pacific PA-1 non-powered engine w/RS, 1992	CP	____
48300	Southern Pacific, boxcar, 1987	35	____
48301	DRGW, boxcar, 1987	35	____
48302	Canadian Pacific, boxcar, 1987	35	____
48303	C & O Chessie System, boxcar, 1987	35	____
48304	Burlington Northern, boxcar, 1987	35	____
48305	Wabash, boxcar, 1988	25	____
48306	Seaboard Coast Line, boxcar, 1988	25	____
48307	Western Pacific, boxcar, 1988	25	____
(4)8308	Maine Central, boxcar, 1990	25	____
(4)8309	American Flyer, boxcar, 1990	31	____
(4)8310	MKT, boxcar, 1991	CP	____
48400	Southern Pacific, tank car, 1987	30	____
48470	JC, NASG, boxcar, 1988	30	____

	Mint Cond / $	
48500 Southern Pacific, gondola, with canisters, 1987	20	______
48501 Southern Pacific, flatcar, with trailers, 1987	25	______
48502 Wabash, flatcar, 1988	25	______
48503 Wabash, gondola w/canisters, 1988	20	______
(4)8505 Illinois Central Gulf, flatcar with bulkheads, 1990	23	______
48600 Southern Pacific, hopper, 1987	20	______
48601 Union Pacific, hopper, 1987	20	______
48602 Erie, hopper with coal load, 1987	22	______
48603 Wabash, hopper, 1988	18	______
48604 Milwaukee Road, hopper, 1988	18	______
48605 BN, hopper, 1988	18	______
48700 Southern Pacific, caboose, 1987	30	______
48701 Illinois Central Gulf, caboose, 1987	30	______
48702 Wabash, caboose, 1988	30	______
48703 Union Pacific, caboose, 1988	30	______
48705 Pennsylvania, caboose, 1989	30	______
(4)8706 BN, caboose, 1990	32	______
(4)8707 New Haven, caboose, 1991	CP	______
48800 Wabash, reefer, 1988	25	______
48801 Union Pacific, reefer, 1988	25	______
48802 Pennsylvania, reefer, 1988	25	______
(4)8805 National Dairy Despatch, boxcar, 1990	30	______
48900 C & O, combination, 1989	50	______
48901 C & O, coach, 1989	50	______
48902 C & O, vista dome, 1989	50	______
48903 C & O, observation, 1989	50	______
(4)8904 UP, combination, 1990	55	______
(4)8905 UP, coach, 1990	55	______
(4)8906 UP, vista dome, 1990	55	______
(4)8907 UP, observation, 1990	55	______
(4)8908 UP, coach, 1990	100	______
(4)8909 UP, vista dome, 1990	100	______
(4)8910 (MP), combination, 1991	CP	______
(4)8911 (MP), vista dome, 1991	CP	______
(4)8912 (MP), coach, 1991	CP	______
(4)8913 (MP), observation, 1991	CP	______
(4)8914 (MP), coach, 1991	CP	______
(4)8915 (MP), vista dome, 1991	CP	______
48925 N P passenger coach, 1992	CP	______
(4)9001 NYC, floodlight car, 1990	29	______
(4)9002 Union Pacific, floodlight car, 1991	CP	______
49006 M R animated caboose, 1992	CP	______
120089 MKT, NASG, tank car, 1989	30	______

CATALOGUES AND MANUALS
Gilbert Production

	Good	Exc	Cond / $
1946			
D1451 Consumer catalogue			
(A) As above	25	100	____
(B) With red binder	NRS	NRS	____
No number Envelope for D1451	3	5	____
D1455 Dealer	25	100	____
D1457 Gilbert scientific toys	10	20	____
D1458 Appointment card	.50	1.50	____
M2499 Instruction sheet	.25	1	____
1947			
D1472 Catalogue	12	50	____
D1473 Consumer catalogue	20	80	____
No number Envelope for D1473	3	5	____
D1482 Dealer catalogue	6	25	____
D1492 Erector Fun and Action	5	15	____
D1495 What Retail Stores Should Know	5	15	____
D1496 Display suggestions	NRS	NRS	____
D1502 Advance catalogue	12	35	____
M2502 Instruction book	2	4	____
1948			
D1505 Advance catalogue	10	30	____
D1507 Consumer catalogue	15	70	____
D1508 Superman	10	60	____
D1508 Consumer catalogue			
(A) As above	10	25	____
(B) Postage Prepaid	5	20	____
1949			
D1525 Bang Bang Torpedo	50	100	____
D1530 Advance catalogue	12	35	____
D1535 Consumer catalogue	NRS	NRS	____
D1536 Consumer catalogue	10	50	____
D1552 How to Sell American Flyer	5	20	____
M2690 Instruction booklet			
(A) Yellow cover	2	5	____
(B) White cover	4	10	____
1950			
D1578 Dealer catalogue	12	50	____
D1579 Gilbert Toys	6	16	____

	Good	Exc	Cond / $
D1581/D1581A Red/blue ad	NRS	NRS	____
D1604 Consumer catalogue	15	50	____
D1629 Dealer Action Displays sheet	NRS	NRS	____
D1631 Dealer TV ad	3	10	____
No number Ready Again booklet	NRS	NRS	____
1951			
D1637 Dealer catalogue	10	25	____
D1637A Advance catalogue	8	25	____
D1640 Consumer catalogue	10	45	____
D1652 Facts About AF Trains	NRS	NRS	____
D1656 AF and Toys	3	6	____
D1660 Gilbert Electric Eye	3	6	____
1952			
D1667 Advance catalogue	13	35	____
D1667A Advance catalogue	10	25	____
D1668A Consumer catalogue	NRS	NRS	____
D1670 Single sheet 200 series bldgs.	3	10	____
D1677 Consumer catalogue	10	40	____
D1678 Facts About AF Trains	5	10	____
M2978 AF Model Railroad Handbook	2	10	____
M2984 Instruction book	1	4	____
No number Advance catalogue	NRS	NRS	____
No Number Consumer catalogue, Spanish	NRS	NRS	____
1953			
D1699 Consumer catalogue	NRS	NRS	____
D1703 Erector and Other Toys	3	6	____
D1704 Dealer catalogue	8	35	____
D1714 Dealer catalogue, East	8	30	____
D1715 Consumer catalogue, West	8	30	____
D1727 Tips on Selling AF Trains	5	10	____
D1728 Tips on Erector	3	9	____
1954			
D1740 Erector and Gilbert Toys	1	5	____
D1744 AF and Erector ad program	5	18	____
D1746 Dealer catalogue			
(A) Pulp	8	20	____
(B) Glossy	8	25	____
D1748 Catalogue, East			
(A) Consumer	3	10	____
(B) Dealer	5	15	____
D1749 Dealer catalogue, West	5	20	____
D1750 Dealer Displays	NRS	NRS	____

		Good	Exc	Cond / $
D1760	Consumer catalogue, East	7	35	
D1761	Consumer catalogue, West	10	25	
D1762	Boys RR Club letter	2	5	
D1769	Read All About Ad Campaign	NRS	NRS	
D1777	Reply postcard	1	3	
M3290	Instruction book	2	5	
	1955			
D1782	Dealer catalogue	6	18	
D1783	Certificate of Registry	2	5	
D1784	Consumer catalogue	NRS	NRS	
D1801	Consumer catalogue, East	5	20	
D1802	Consumer catalogue, West	8	20	
D1814	Choo Choo Sound foldout	1	5	
D1816	Dealer catalogue	10	25	
D1820	HO consumer catalogue	1	3	
D1835	Tips for Selling Erector	1	3	
D1840	Envelope	1	5	
M3450	Instruction book	1	4	
	1956			
D1866	Consumer catalogue, East	6	25	
D1867	Consumer catalogue, West	6	25	
D1874	Dealer catalogue	12	35	
D1879	Gilbert and Erector Toys	1	7	
D1882	AF and Erector Displays	1	7	
D1899	Consumer catalogue	NRS	NRS	
D1904	Gilbert HO catalogue	NRS	NRS	
D1907	Dealer catalogue	6	25	
D1920	How to Build a Model Railroad	2	10	
D1922	Miniature catalogue	6	25	
D1925	Erector folder	2	8	
D1926	Envelope for D1922 catalogue	2	5	
	1957			
D1937	Dealer catalogue	7	15	
D1966	Consumer catalogue	2	8	
D1973	Erector and Other Toys	1	3	
D1980	Cardboard	NRS	NRS	
D1981	Same as D1980	NRS	NRS	
D2006	Consumer catalogue, East	8	20	
D2007	Consumer catalogue, West	10	25	
D2008	Erector and Toys	1	5	
D2022	Dealer flyer	NRS	NRS	
D2031	Consumer catalogue	NRS	NRS	
D2037	Erector and Gilbert Toys	1	6	
D2045	Gilbert promotion kit	NRS	NRS	

		Good	Exc	Cond / $
M3817	HO instructions	2	8	_____
M4195	Instruction sheet	2	6	_____
No number	Same as M3450 (1955) but w/o number	NRS	NRS	_____

1958

		Good	Exc	Cond / $
D2047	Consumer catalogue	20	80	_____
D2048	Catalogue, West	25	70	_____
D2058	Erector and Toys	1	5	_____
D2060	Erector and Gilbert Toys	2	10	_____
D2073	Advance catalogue	5	15	_____
D2080	Smoking caboose	NRS	NRS	_____
D2086	Consumer folder, East	3	15	_____
D2087	Consumer folder, West	1	10	_____
D2088	Consumer folder	3	15	_____
D2101	Career Building Science Toys	1	3	_____
D4106	HO catalogue	2	5	_____
M4195	Accessory folder	2	6	_____
M4202	Color billboards	NRS	NRS	_____

1959

		Good	Exc	Cond / $
D2115	Dealer catalogue	8	35	_____
No Number	Canadian, D2115	NRS	NRS	_____
D2118	AF No. 20142, Willit	NRS	NRS	_____
D2120	Career Building Science Toys	1	5	_____
D2125	Overland Express sheet	1	3	_____
D2146	Consumer catalogue	1	5	_____
D2148	Consumer catalogue	1	5	_____
D2171-D2179	Dealer promotional set	NRS	NRS	_____
D2179	Promotional sheet, Franklin Set	1	5	_____
D2180	Gilbert Science Toys	1	5	_____
No Number	Catalogue, Gilbert toys	NRS	NRS	_____
M4225	Train assembly and operating instructions	NRS	NRS	_____
M4326	Accessory catalogue	1	3	_____
M4869	AF Maintenance Manual	1	3	_____

1960

		Good	Exc	Cond / $
D2192	Catalogue			
	(A) Dealer	6	15	_____
	(B) Advance	NRS	NRS	_____
D2193	Consumer catalogue	2	8	_____
D2193REV	Revised consumer catalogue	2	8	_____
D2198	Action and Fun catalogue	2	6	_____
D2205	Gilbert Toys	1	3	_____
D2208	Dealer advance catalogue	NRS	NRS	_____
D2223	Gilbert Science Toys	1	4	_____

		Good	Exc	Cond / $
D2224	Consumer folder	2	8	____
D2225	Consumer folder	2	5	____
D2226	Consumer folder	1	4	____
D2230	Consumer catalogue	7	30	____
D2231	Consumer catalogue	3	10	____
No Number	Promotional sheet, Truscott Set	NRS	NRS	____
	1961			
D2238	Career Building Science Toys	3	15	____
D2239	Consumer catalogue	3	15	____
D2242REV	Auto Rama catalogue	.50	2	____
D2255	1961-62 retail display	.50	2	____
D2266	Gilbert Science Toys	1	5	____
D2267	Consumer catalogue	3	15	____
D2268	Folder, Auto Rama folder	.50	2	____
	1962			
No number	The Big Ones Come From Gilbert	NRS	NRS	____
D2277REV	Career Building Science Toys	8	25	____
D2278	Dealer catalogue	NRS	NRS	____
D2278REV	Revised dealer catalogue	2	10	____
D2282	Dealer catalogue	NRS	NRS	____
D2282	Consumer catalogue	4	10	____
D2283	HO trains and accessories	2	8	____
D2307	Consumer Ad Mats	NRS	NRS	____
D2310	Consumer catalogue	3	15	____
M6874	Instruction booklet	1	5	____
	1963			
D2321	Dealer catalogue	2	5	____
D2321REV	Revised dealer catalogue	5	20	____
D2328	Consumer catalogue	NRS	NRS	____
X863-3	Consumer catalogue	2	12	____
	1964			
X-264-6	Consumer catalogue	3	15	____
No Number	Similar to X-264-6, 8 pages	NRS	NRS	____
No Number	Similar to X-264-6, black binding	NRS	NRS	____
564-11	Dealer catalogue	2	8	____
	1965			
X165-12	Dealer catalogue	7	15	____

	Good	Exc	Cond / $
X165-12REV Revised dealer catalogue	7	15	______
X365-10 Consumer folder	2	5	______
T465-5REV Dealer folder	1	3	______
1966			
T-166-6 Dealer catalogue	3	9	______
T166-7 Gilbert Action Toys	5	25	______
X-466-1 Consumer catalogue	3	12	______
M6788 All Aboard instructions	2	8	______
1967			
No number Four-page folder	1	5	______

CATALOGUES AND MANUALS
Lionel Production, 1979-1991

		Like New	Cond / $
	1979		
No number	Consumer catalogue	5	_____
	1980		
No number	Consumer catalogue	3	_____
	1981		
No number	Consumer catalogue	3	_____
	1982		
No number	Consumer catalogue	3	_____
	1983		
No number	Consumer catalogue	2	_____
	1984		
No number	Consumer catalogue	2	_____
	1985		
No number	Consumer catalogue	2	_____
	1986		
No number	Consumer catalogue	2	_____
	1987		
No number	Dealer catalogue	2	_____
	1988		
No number	Dealer catalogue	2	_____
No number	Dealer catalogue	2	_____
	1989		
No number	Dealer catalogue	2	_____
	1990		
No number	Dealer catalogue, Book One	2	_____
No number	Dealer catalogue, Book Two	2	_____
	1991		
No number	Dealer catalogue, Book Two	2	_____

NOTES

NOTES

Railroad Name Abbreviations

A F (A F L)	American Flyer (Lines)
A R T Co.	American Refrigerator Transit Co.
A T S F	Atchison, Topeka & Santa Fe
B A R	Bangor & Aroostook Railroad
B M	Boston and Maine
B N	Burlington Northern
B & O	Baltimore & Ohio
C B & Q	Chicago, Burlington, & Quincy
C & E I	Chicago & Eastern Illinois
C of G	Central of Georgia
C M St P & P	Chicago, Milwaukee, St. Paul and Pacific
C N	Canadian National
C N W	Chicago North Western
C & N W RY	Chicago & North Western Railway
C & O	Chesapeake & Ohio
C R P	Jersey Central Lines
D & H	Delware & Hudson
D R G	Denver & Rio Grande
D R G W	Denver & Rio Grande Western
F Y & P	Fifty Years of Progress
F Y & P R R	Fifty Years of Progress in Railroading
G A E X	General American Express
G M	General Motors
G N	Great Northern
I C	Illinois Central
L & N	Louisville & Nashville
L N E	Lehigh New England
M E C	Maine Central
M K T	Missouri-Kansas-Texas
M P	Missouri Pacific
M R	Milwaukee Road
M St L	Missouri & St. Louis
N A S G	National Association of S-Gaugers
N H	New Haven
N K P	Nickel Plate Road
N P	Northern Pacific
N W	North Western
N & W	Norfolk & Western
N Y C	New York Central
N Y N H & H	New York, New Haven, and Hartford
P R R	Pennsylvania Railroad
R L	Reading Lines
S F	Santa Fe
S P	Southern Pacific
T & P	Texas & Pacific
U F G E	United Fruit Growers Express
U P	Union Pacific
U S A F	United States Air Force
U S M	United States Marines
W S X	White's Discount Centers

Abbreviations

The following is a list of abbreviations used throughout this Pocket Guide:

* — excellent reproductions made
AC — alternating current
bldgs. — buildings
comb. — combination
Cond — condition
DC — direct current
EMD — Electro Motive Division of GM
FP — diesel locomotive
gen. — generator
GP — diesel locomotive
Jct. — Junction
KC — knuckle couplers
lett. — lettering
LH — left hand
mv — many variations
oper. — operating
PA — Alco diesel w/cab
pass. — passenger
PB — Alco diesel w/o cab
PM — Pike Master
ptd. — painted
QE — questionable existence
RC — remote control
REV — revised
RH — right hand
sib. — smoke in boiler
sit. — smoke in tender
sta. — station
(U) — Uncatalogued
Wash. — Washington
West. — Western